THE I.T. TRAINER'S P

C000279045

By Jooli Atkins

Drawings by Phil Hailstone

"A fabulous journey through all aspects of IT training - full of creative ideas and helpful hints. Will help ensure both you and your learners get the most from any learning event. Don't leave home without it!"
Michelle Mook, Training Consultant and IT Training Manager for York Hospitals NHS Trust

"Many years of experience and understanding of the IT training arena are shared here in this pocketbook. It provides simple tips with clear, succinct explanations that will accelerate the effectiveness of any IT trainer – in an environment which is creative and fun to be in for both trainer and learner."
Sarah Nelmes, IT Training Professional

Published by:
Management Pocketbooks Ltd
Laurel House, Station Approach, Alresford, Hants SO24 9JH, U.K.
Tel: +44 (0)1962 735573   Fax: +44 (0)1962 733637
E-mail: sales@pocketbook.co.uk
Website: www.pocketbook.co.uk

This edition published 2003. Reprinted 2007.

British Library Cataloguing-in-Publication Data – A catalogue record for this book is available from the British Library.

ISBN   978 1 903776 124

Design, typesetting and graphics by **efex ltd**   Printed in U.K.

CONTENTS

AUTHOR'S INTRODUCTION

For the purposes of this book and to simplify understanding (both mine and yours) the word *application* is used to describe a computer application, operating system or back-office tool, regardless of its platform or use.

As the purpose of the book is to consider issues surrounding IT training, *what* is being trained should be almost irrelevant. Where there are specific differences to be dealt with, they will be identified at the time.

ADULT LEARNERS

STARTING AT THE VERY BEGINNING

Before any learning event it is important to establish not only **what** the learners need, but **why** such a need has been identified.

Learning should always be linked to a business need and, although few IT trainers are involved in identifying that need, it is important that you are aware of it in order firmly to anchor the benefits for the learners.

The overall outcome of the training may be identified by others, but it is often the trainer's job to identify the individual's existing skills, the current gap between existing and required skills and the best route for the individual to bridge that gap.

TRAINING NEEDS ANALYSIS

The identification of the training required can be carried out using a number of techniques, often named **Training Needs Analysis**. The main tools used to carry out TNAs are:

- Testing
- Questionnaires
- Discussion

Testing
There are numerous testing programmes on the market that require the learner to carry out specific processes using actual or simulated software applications. Although they can be useful in identifying specific skills, they are of little use to people who do not have the IT skills necessary to carry out the test. Also, they can be intimidating if used as the sole identification method. Another issue connected with their use is the demotivating effect of some software that restricts the learner to the 'right way' which may not reflect their preferred way of doing something.

TRAINING NEEDS ANALYSIS

Questionnaires

Questionnaires designed to ask questions like: '*Do you know how to send an e-mail?*' are often used to identify needs. Again, they are useful, to an extent. One of the limitations of this tool is that to be able to answer the questions accurately the learner needs to speak the same, often technical, language as the question writer and they can often under- or over-estimate their own skills.

If generic skills are required, questions like the one above are useful, but if more specific skills need to be assessed a detailed multiple-choice questionnaire might be better. Whichever method is used with questionnaires, it is a good idea to ask the learner's manager, subordinate and/or peer to complete it at the same time, as this 360° analysis provides far more useful information.

TRAINING NEEDS ANALYSIS

Discussion

Discussion is by far the most valuable means of evaluating needs, providing both quantitative and qualitative analysis when done properly. It allows for questions to be asked: *'Do you know how to send an e-mail?'*, skills to be tested: *'Please will you show me how you do that?'* and business context to be ascertained: *'Please tell me about three situations when you would send an e-mail.'*.

This type of discussion can only be really effective if it is structured correctly. If the analysis is being used to formulate a structured training programme and make sure that people with the same skills are on the same course, it should be consistent.

LEARNING CYCLE

In 1975 David Kolb and Roger Fry identified a model for experiential learning which they named the Learning Cycle.

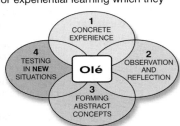

- Although learning can begin at any of the points on the cycle, it commonly begins with a person carrying out a particular action
- The second step is to look at and understand the effects of the action in the circumstances in which it took place
- The third step is then to understand the general principle (rule of thumb) of the effects in order to transfer the learning to different circumstances
- Finally, the action is tested under new circumstances to see whether the general principles and understanding are correct. This inevitably leads to someone carrying out an action and the process begins again

Process around this cycle leads to the Overall Learning Experience (OLÉ).

LEARNING CYCLE IN I.T. TRAINING

Each learning point needs to be experienced, reflected upon, generalised and tested.
Eg: in a spreadsheet course when training users to use an
automatic sum tool to add a column of figures:

1. **Experience**: they click the sum tool button, then
   select the relevant data, if necessary, and press
   ENTER
2. **Reflection**: they consider what happened when
   the sum tool button was pressed and how this
   process affected the data
3. **Rule of thumb**: they conclude that if they needed to
   add a different set of numbers, they could move to a
   relevant cell and click the sum tool button
4. **Testing**: they test out their theory with a different set of numbers

However simple this may appear, the same model can be used in a variety of ways and,
provided the cycle is gone through in its entirety, learning is likely to occur.

(11)

LEARNING STYLES

Peter Honey and Alan Mumford in 1982 identified four learning styles, which map onto Kolb and Fry's learning cycle.

It is useful to know that some people may have a preference for a particular learning style. I am an Activist, for example, and that means that I prefer to learn by doing rather than thinking too much about what I have done. The danger for me is to think that I can *only* learn by doing and forget about the other stages of the cycle.

In any learning event, all learners should be encouraged, despite any preference they may have, to go right round the cycle to gain fully from the event.

ENGAGING THE DIFFERENT STYLES

Regardless of an individual's preference, it is possible to engage everyone in an event and ensure that each style has sufficient '**What's in it for me?**' from the learning by following the learning cycle:

- Do **IT**
- Think about **IT**
- Draw conclusions from **IT**
- Plan what else you can do with **IT**

SENSORY THINKING STYLES

We are all aware of our senses to a greater or lesser extent. Some of us prefer to represent the world (think) using one or other of our senses.

There are three ways of 'sensory thinking':

- Visual – seeing
- Auditory – hearing
- Kinaesthetic – feeling (this incorporates touch, taste and smell)

The way a message is interpreted can be affected, therefore, by the way it is delivered. For example, if you introduce a new topic visually by writing or drawing on a flipchart or an overhead, it will be processed most effectively by those people who prefer to process visually. Although it is unlikely that people who have a stronger alternative preference will ignore the message, it is not going to be processed as effectively as if you had found a way of accessing all three senses.

Recognising that someone has a particularly strong preference can be a useful skill for a trainer.

ADULT LEARNERS

RECOGNISING SENSORY PREFERENCES

The aim is to become skilled at detecting another person's preference and then using it to communicate.

People give clues about their preferences in their language:

Visual
- Look ....
- I see what you mean
- I get the picture
- I see

Auditory
- Listen ...
- That sounds good
- I hear what you are saying
- That rings a bell

Kinaesthetic
- Hold on ...
- I get the drift
- I think I have grasped that
- I am getting to grips with it

RECOGNISING SENSORY PREFERENCES

People also give clues by the direction in which their eyes move and the speed of their speech when thinking:

Visual
- Eyes tend to drift upwards and they speak quickly

Auditory
- Eyes tend to look to the side or straight ahead – speech is reasonably paced

Kinaesthetic
- Eyes tend to move downwards – speech is slow and careful. Beware thinking that this is an indicator of lack of interest.

Remember when teachers used to say, *'Look at me, not your boots'*? For kinaesthetic thinkers, the answer may well be in their boots, just as visual thinkers can often find the answer on the ceiling!

ADULT LEARNERS

DIGITAL THINKING

There is also a fourth language pattern which indicates a thinking style that does not fit into any of the visual, auditory or kinaesthetic styles. Known as 'digital', it does not stem from any sensory preference but from non-sensory preference. Digital thinking involves a focus on the facts and/or the use of data and statistics.

Digital Clues
- Please explain …
- The fact is …
- The statistics prove …
- In fact …

Think of Spock and Data in *Star Trek*.

Most business writing (particularly technical writing such as IT training courseware) is in the digital style. As there are relatively few digital thinkers compared with those of us who use our senses, it is probably the least effective way of communicating to the majority of the intended audience.

USING ALL THE SENSES

No learner will have just one thinking style – they probably have a dominant preference and mix that with at least one of the others.

Good trainers **blend** their training and are excellent at:

- Seeing things from another perspective
- Hearing how it sounds to someone else
- Going to where they are at
- Keeping it simple and succinct

Remember the other three senses to round off the whole event:

- Sixth Sense – intuition is a powerful tool
- Common Sense – remember to keep it with you at all times
- Nonsense – avoid it at all costs

do unto others as they would have you do unto them.

The secret to excellent communication is to …

APPROACHES TO LEARNING

Knowles et al (1984) distinguished between the traditional teaching experience we usually associate with school (pedagogic) and the learning we do as an adult (androgogic) in the following ways:

Pedagogy
- Treating the learner as if they were a child or an empty vessel to be filled
- Preparing the curriculum in advance without negotiation with the learner
- Teaching the prepared course while maintaining the learner in a dependent condition and relatively powerless

Pedagogy derives from the Greek *paidagogos*, a slave who took children to and from school and was, it is assumed, responsible for ensuring that they learned what was expected of them.

ADULT LEARNERS

APPROACHES TO LEARNING

Androgogy

- Treating the learner as an adult, co-learning with the teacher; appreciating the prior experience of the learner in connection with future learning
- Negotiating the curriculum with the learner to allow for consultation and involvement in the learning process
- Empowering the learner to take control of their own learning
- Interacting with the teacher in a co-operative, sharing environment

PEDAGOGY OR ANDROGOGY?

Many IT certification routes have a prepared curriculum and many learners appear to have no prior experience of the subject (empty vessel).

Even under these circumstances, however, it is possible, through interaction, to consult and involve the learner in the learning process. This in itself can empower the learner to take control of their own learning.

An appreciation of the prior experience of the learner is also essential – they will undoubtedly know more than they think they know. It is the trainer's job to help them to understand that they do know and encourage them to build on their existing knowledge and skills in a new direction.

More important than either of these general theories is the knowledge that **each learner is individual within the group** and will only learn successfully when all of his or her individual needs are met – a tall order for any trainer but worth aspiring to.

MULTIPLE INTELLIGENCES

Dr Howard Gardner defined eight intelligences that we can use in the training room to help people learn in a way or ways in which they are naturally talented.

- **Verbal-linguistic** learners enjoy words and activities that involve speaking, listening, reading or creative writing.
- **Logical-mathematical** learners enjoy abstract themes, calculations or problems.

Most learning events appeal to these two intelligences, but few allow learners to use the others identified by Gardner, which are detailed on the next two pages.

MULTIPLE INTELLIGENCES (Cont'd)

- **Musical** learners enjoy rhythms, singing and musical sounds.
- **Spatial** learners enjoy model-making, drawing, mind maps and the use of colour.
- **Bodily kinaesthetic** learners gain from using their body in some physical way perhaps by throwing a ball, moving around the room, role-playing and dancing.
- **Inter-personal** learners enjoy their relationship with others, and work well in a group, batting ideas around and collaborating to achieve results.
- **Intra-personal** learners benefit from reflection, particularly self-reflection, and prefer to have thinking time built into training sessions.

MULTIPLE INTELLIGENCES (Cont'd)

- **Naturalist** learners relate to the natural world and although it is difficult to deliver an IT learning event outdoors, it is possible to bring some of the natural world indoors to help these learners.

Being creative about your use of these multiple intelligences, together with consideration of sensory preferences and learning styles, will make the overall learning event more memorable and, therefore, more effective for a large number of people.

HOW I.T. TRAINING IS <u>DIFFERENT</u>

TECHNOLOGY: BE PREPARED

The technology being trained is often a major area of concern to IT trainers. Will it work? No matter how many times it has before, today is the day that it won't! The key to any successful IT training event is preparation. Expect things to go wrong, eg:

PC unavailable – Have back-up exercises that can be done without a PC while you arrange for a replacement through the IT department contact you need to have made prior to the event.

More people than PCs – Consider your options. Must each person have a PC, or can they share (if they agree to)? If sharing is an option, make sure that the same people do not share throughout. Rotate the sharing, but not the extra person.

It is important, here, to consider *why* more people turned up. Is the administration side of the business inefficient, or has the business side sent extra people because they don't understand how this affects the training? Perhaps someone has come because she has a free day today and won't be able to make the session already planned for her at a later date! Each reason has a different effect on the person to be trained.

TECHNOLOGY: BE PREPARED

Data projector unavailable/unusable – We depend more and more on data projectors as visual aids, but what happens if it is not working or blows a bulb? Few organisations have spare bulbs just lying around.

Once again, you need to be aware of the route for organising replacement or repair, or have an alternative strategy. If you are using presentation software, always prepare a paper copy in case it is needed. If you are using a data projector to demonstrate (anti-demonstration, of course – see page 78), you can arrange the group so that they can adequately see a PC and ask for a volunteer to carry out the demonstration, with your guidance. If this situation lasts for most of the day, rotate your demonstrators to ensure participation.

TECHNOLOGY: BE PREPARED

PCs installed with wrong version, or even wrong software – If it is the wrong version, consider the differences. You might be able to start with this version and then arrange for a longer break while the PCs are amended. If it is the wrong software altogether, you really can't start the software part of the training at all, but you can do introductory work, discussing the software and its benefits to individuals while the correct version is being installed.

Of course, you will have discovered the problem quite early, as it is one of the first things you will check when you arrive in the training room. But it may be difficult to organise if there is no one in the IT department to change it for you until 9 am. Come clean with the learners. They will sense a problem and may begin to make up their own version of what's wrong if you don't tell them.

Do take care how you break this news, however, as you may make the IT department, training department or the organisation look disorganised, which is not what you want.

HOW MUCH KNOWLEDGE?

Personal preparation is also essential. One area of concern is how much you need to know about an application to be able to train someone else. The answer is (as is so often the case) *'it depends'*. Of course, you need to know the content of what you are training. From then on, your effectiveness as a trainer can be increased in a number of ways.

It is reasonable, for example, for someone training advanced spreadsheets to have little or no knowledge of the maths behind a function that allows the user to return the inverse of the gamma cumulative distribution! Much more important than detailed knowledge of all areas of an application is **real-life experience** of using it. Knowing *how* something works and knowing *why* you would want it to, are very different things!

Don't worry about not knowing the answer to a learner's question; help them to find the answer for themselves. It is quite reassuring for learners to realise that the 'expert' does not know all of the answers and it is incredibly empowering for them to learn how to find out. And remember, this is not a knowledge competition. It is all about facilitating *their* learning not increasing *your* self-assurance.

HOW I.T. TRAINING IS DIFFERENT

PRE-COURSE KNOWLEDGE FORMULA

Use this formula to identify your knowledge before a learning event:

$$K = C \times (C + R + B/2) + A$$

Knowledge = **C**ontent x (**C**ontent + **R**eal-life experience + **B**usiness understanding/2) + **A**dditional content

B is halved, because at preparation stage your maximum business understanding is half of the actual business needs of your learners. This assumes that you have not done the same job as them for the same length of time and in the same depth – a likely assumption! It is only while working with them on the course itself that you can get close to gaining the other half.

Example: (*Where the maximum score given to any element is 10*)

Content = 10 (you should always know the content)   Real-life experience = 2
Business understanding = 3   Additional content = 10

Here, real-life experience and business understanding are relatively low, but you have prepared twice as much content as you need. Therefore, your maximum knowledge is 145, being 56% of the possible maximum of 260.

PRE-COURSE KNOWLEDGE FORMULA

Compare the previous example to one where the additional content is low, but you have some real-life experience of using the initial content, combined with some understanding of the business issues facing the learners:

Content = 10 (again, you should always know the content)
Real-life experience = 6   Business understanding = 5   Additional content = 3

Your knowledge score has increased to 188, 72% of the possible maximum.

This formula shows that the mix of real-life and business understanding is significantly more important than additional content knowledge. Equally, lack of real-life and business understanding can have a dramatic effect on your knowledge.

My belief is that no one should attempt to train a course without at least a 50% score. Using the formula, this can't be achieved without at least 7 in content, even with 10s in real-life and business awareness and 0 in additional content (if you can't get the content, you are unlikely to have additional content). This should only be considered as a very last resort, perhaps when a colleague is ill and you have to take over at the last minute.

I.T. USED AS DELIVERY METHOD

It is easy to rely on IT as a delivery tool in IT training. With data projectors available in most training rooms, the temptation to demonstrate learners to death is very high.

It is useful for learners to be able to see what they are aiming towards, but data projectors and PCs should only be used as visual aids, not as the learning delivery method.

We will discuss online learning and the effective use of demonstrations in another section of this book.

HOW I.T. TRAINING IS DIFFERENT

JARGON

Techno-jargon? In Yorkshire, we just 'tech-no-notice'!

The IT industry is one of the most jargon-filled. Add to that organisation-specific jargon and you often have confused and intimidated learners. It feels as though the whole world is full of TLAs (three letter acronyms).

There is an argument for not using any jargon in training, but this is not one I subscribe to. There is, however, one rule I hold to and that is to DAA (define all acronyms).

Balancing the jargon by using it, while explaining its use, is the best way forward. It is important for learners to be aware of jargon, particularly application users who may have to speak to helpdesks, as ability to use technical terms can increase their confidence when talking to IT professionals.

Understanding and using jargon appropriately, with the emphasis on *appropriate* use, should be part of the learning process. Use jargon to enhance the learner's confidence, not undermine it. It is not a competition to see who can make the most four-letter words out of Transmission Control Protocol Internet Protocol (TCPIP)!

HOW I.T. TRAINING IS DIFFERENT

'DIFFICULT' DELEGATES

For some learners, the fact that they are attending an IT training course is akin to asking them to do role play on a course – they hate the idea because they feel that they will be made to look silly.

Other people enjoy the opportunity to show off their IT skills, particularly to colleagues who may be feeling less skilled. This can be equally difficult to handle.

There is no such thing as a 'difficult' delegate, just difficult behaviour. Their behaviour in the training room may be difficult to deal with but it is often a symptom of how they are feeling. The skill in dealing with such behaviour is to find out *why* they are behaving in that way and then deal with it appropriately.

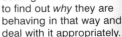

'DIFFICULT' DELEGATES

WHO IS THE BEHAVIOUR DIFFICULT FOR?

Before deciding how you might manage the difficult behaviour, consider who the behaviour is proving difficult for:

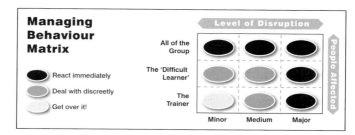

When using this matrix, ask yourself the following questions:

- Should I intervene at all?

- Would intervening be worse than the difficult behaviour?

- If intervening is necessary: - What will I do? - When will I do it? - Where will I do it?

'DIFFICULT' DELEGATES

KNOW IT ALL

The Know It All is a very useful asset in the training room – that is, if she really does know it all! But if that really is the case, why is she there? If you truly have someone who knows it all and can prove this to you (make sure that you check, through exercises and questions) there really is little point in her staying if she would prefer not to. Check with the individual and the course organisers to find out if they are happy for Know It All to return to work before sending her packing. It may be that she has been sent for a particular topic that is crucial for her development.

If Know It All decides to stay, you can ask her to help you by offering advice and experience on the topic under discussion **when asked** (be warned: Know It All may attempt to take over if you do not handle the situation carefully). Few people would turn down the opportunity of having their skills paraded in this way and if managed well this can be of great benefit to both you and the learners. After all, without Know It All, all the learners can get is *your* point of view on topics new to them.

'DIFFICULT' DELEGATES

KNOW IT ALL (Cont'd)

But what if Know It All only *thinks* she knows it? You can, in fact, use the same technique to great effect …

'Jenny, you have clearly had lots of experience of this topic. What are your thoughts on Simon's question?'

This acknowledges Jenny's expertise, which she will find very flattering in front of her colleagues, and she will do one of two things – either offer some gem of experience because she really does know it, or waffle and become embarrassed by the question. She may also shut up, which is usually the solution to the difficult behaviour of a Know It All – they never shut up. Even if she tries to waffle her way through the question, she is less likely to be vocal about her talents in the future if she thinks that you might ask her to elaborate on something she knows nothing about.

37

'DIFFICULT' DELEGATES

TECHNOPHOBE

Some people are just downright terrified of IT. They hear the jargon, see the anoraks and feel afraid, feel very afraid. I have a theory that such people suffer from anoraknophobia! Of course, the definition of a phobia is an irrational fear and this is often the case with Technophobes.

Technophobes have difficulty seeing any benefit to IT systems, but focus on the threat they appear to pose. Stressing the benefits on an individual basis is the key to getting them on board. They need to know exactly how each piece of information is going to help them to do their jobs or live their lives more easily and fully. Open their eyes to the science that is currently blinding them, by breaking it down into bite-sized chunks and stressing little victories, making real the benefits as early as possible.

Don't avoid using jargon, but clearly explain the more common uses to increase confidence and use. Keep it light and fun where possible, as some of the jargon regularly used is actually quite silly when you think about it. How can anyone feel threatened when they realise that they have just learned to drag and drop in a GUI?

HOW I.T. TRAINING IS DIFFERENT

'DIFFICULT' DELEGATES

FIDDLER

The Fiddler may appear to be out to get you, but he is probably just learning in a way that suits his style. Activists prefer to learn by doing, making mistakes along the way as part of the process. This can be hard to deal with when you are trying to describe something to an attentive group with an activist learner *playing* at the back of the room.

The answer is to make sure that a Fiddler always has something to do, preferably something of your choice rather than his. Involve him at all times – as flipchart scribe when you discuss the benefits of a particular feature, or ask him to hand out the exercise sheets while the other, more reflective, learners are thinking about what they have learned in preparation for the exercise.

It often doesn't matter what Fiddler does, as long as he is doing something, because left to his own devices he can potentially do some damage.

And whatever you do, don't tell a Fiddler **not** to do something – it is a bit like telling someone not to press that red button. *'Which red button? This one here?..... Oops!'*

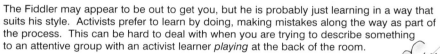

39

REASON FOR LEARNING

Learners' motivation to learn IT skills may have less of a personal development focus than a task focus. This can be linked to organisational change, eg: a systems installation or upgrade, or to a job role change which may include using new IT tools or existing tools differently.

Learners may have many desired outcomes (eg: qualification, product-specific or job-specific) and these will affect their motivation.

Qualification

A specific qualification could be the main purpose for undergoing training, such as:

- MCSE (Microsoft Certified Systems Engineer)
- ITQ (an IT specific National Vocational Qualification)
- MOS (Microsoft Office Specialist)

In this case, the training content is firmly based around the qualification success criteria, whether that is an exam or portfolio. The added value element for learners with this motivation is the *real-life* experience you can offer as a trainer.

REASON FOR LEARNING

Product-specific

Your learner may simply want to know a particular product in detail. There may be no qualification available, or qualification is a more expensive option, but the learning requirement is similar. Focusing on the real-life business use of the product adds value.

Job-specific

Often learners are faced with a specific task, or series of tasks, they need to carry out which may involve the use of more than one product. Eg, a learner may have been asked to research a topic and then present an analysis of the results. This might involve internet searching skills, use of a spreadsheet for analysis and, finally, presentation of the results using a presentation tool. An in-depth knowledge of each of these is unnecessary – just sufficient knowledge to be able to carry out the tasks involved. Additional content can get in the way when learners are task-focused in this way.

Of course, few learners have only one requirement, so it is likely that, as a trainer, you will cover a product feature and its real-world benefits as well as letting learners know about qualifications they might like to consider.

HOW I.T. TRAINING IS DIFFERENT

PREREQUISITE KNOWLEDGE

LIKELY SCENARIOS

One of the biggest headaches for IT trainers is having a mix of learners with a mix of pre-existing skills, experience and abilities on the same course. Naturally, this occurs in other areas of training, but it rarely has the potential impact that it does in IT training. Two real-life scenarios follow with examples of how they might be dealt with.

Scenario 1: Advanced Spreadsheet course – six people

- Four learners tell you that they attended the Introductory course
- One tells you that she has been working with spreadsheets for two years
- One tells you that he has not worked with spreadsheets before and has been sent on the Advanced course by his manager because there is insufficient time for him to attend two courses, and he needs to know about some advanced functions covered on the Advanced course

PREREQUISITE KNOWLEDGE

LIKELY SCENARIOS

Options for Scenario 1

- Start by testing that what they have told you is true, by setting an exercise that they should be able to complete before moving on. Make sure that during the exercise you check *how* they carry out tasks as well as that they get the 'answer' right. This will give you lots of information about their skill levels and the opportunity to coach individuals to an acceptable starting point. It may be that their skills are not as far apart as it first appeared.

- Find out what other applications they have each been using – although one person has not worked with spreadsheets before, he may work in a logical, methodical environment, using mathematical formulae regularly. His aptitude could, therefore, allow you to introduce a short recap session for everyone to bring his skills to an acceptable standard.

- If it becomes clear that he is on the wrong course, you may decide to offer alternative learning opportunities, either to bring his skills to the required standard for him to attend on another date, or to give him the particular skill he needs to learn now.

HOW I.T. TRAINING IS DIFFERENT

PREREQUISITE KNOWLEDGE

LIKELY SCENARIOS

Scenario 2: Technical Operating System course – 10 people
- Six learners are working at an expected pace
- Two are moving ahead, becoming restless and impatient with the others
- Two are struggling to keep up

Options for Scenario 2
- Consider 'buddying' the learners who are working at a different pace from the majority. Beware partnering a fast-paced learner with someone slower. That can lead to even more frustration for both. Instead, partner them with someone of compatible pace. This is reassuring for the slower-paced as they do not feel alienated and can help each other at their own pace. It also allows for the faster-paced learners to move on with additional, challenging exercises. They could also work on real-life scenarios together, allowing them to experiment with new techniques in a safe environment.

ENVIRONMENT

The mere fact that IT training involves the use of IT hardware in some form or another automatically incorporates a barrier between you and the learners. This is often compounded by the use of a classroom-style room layout.

Room Layout

Health and safety issues need considering when designing an IT training room. For advice see the Health and Safety Executive leaflet INDG36 (rev 1).

Workstations

Make sure that learners have made themselves comfortable. As a guide, the forearms should be approximately horizontal and the eyes at the same height as the top of the VDU, with feet flat on the floor or on a footrest. You may wish to provide a wrist rest for keyboard use.

Position monitors in front of the user (rather than having the learner sitting at an angle), avoiding glare and, where possible, not obscuring vision of the trainer, other learners and visual aids. Use anti-glare screens if necessary, making sure that the learner can adjust the monitor settings.

HOW I.T. TRAINING IS DIFFERENT

ENVIRONMENT

During a learning event, encourage learners to take regular breaks from the workstation and move around. This has a number of benefits in addition to the health and safety benefits (see Facilitating Learning, p87 onwards).

PCs

Make sure that PC base units are located in the safest position in relation to the learners and trainer, while checking that it is easy to access power and network points without cables causing a hazard. Where cables are unavoidable, use strong tape or rubber cable protectors to prevent accidents.

Avoid vividly coloured PC software display settings on training machines, as this can cause difficulties for some learners. Where a learner has a particular need in relation to settings (such as large fonts to assist those with visual impairments) these should be made available.

ENVIRONMENT

Decorating the training room
For some obscure reason, most training rooms are decorated with only magnolia or pale green paint. This is not likely to stimulate exciting brain activity, but can provide a backdrop for learners' flipcharts, exercises, drawings, ideas, Post-it notes as well as trainers' reinforcing messages, quotes, drawings, etc. Don't forget that there is also a ceiling that can be used for hanging mobiles carrying reinforcing words and visuals. When people are thinking, they often look up and it would be far more useful for them to see stimulating reinforcement of the learning than to see off-white blocks of fireproofing!

What goes where?
There are pros, cons and considerations involved in most room layouts. The next pages show some examples.

CLASSROOM LAYOUT

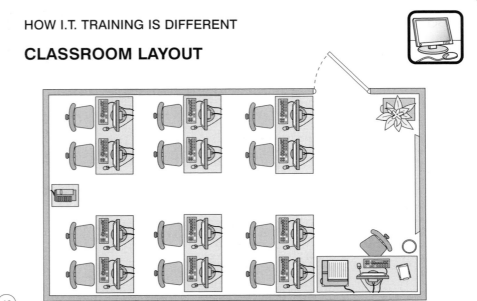

CLASSROOM LAYOUT

Pros
- Accommodates large numbers easily
- Good for working in pairs
- Usually easy access to power/network points
- Naturally front-facing focus

Cons
- Reminds learners of school and the teacher/pupil environment
- Can limit interaction
- PCs provide physical barrier between trainer and learner
- Learners suffer obscured vision unless focused on PC in front
- Difficult to monitor learners' activities
- Difficult to offer discreet one-to-one coaching
- Easy for 'keyboard fiddlers' to hide at the back
- Learners can lean back into PC or monitor behind, posing a health and safety hazard

HORSESHOE LAYOUT

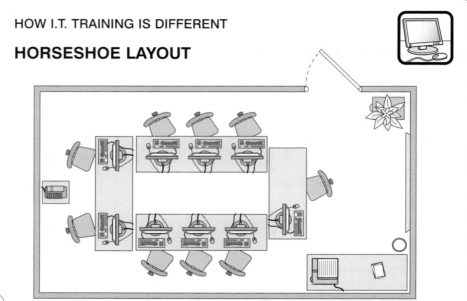

HOW I.T. TRAINING IS DIFFERENT

HORSESHOE LAYOUT

Pros
- Collaborative environment
- Easy to provide one-to-one coaching
- Easy to monitor learners' activities
- Learners have more room to manoeuvre

Cons
- Limited interaction due to physical barriers between trainer and learners
- Often, limited space for trainer to move around
- Power and network points need to be in the middle of the space to avoid health and safety hazard

INSIDE LAYOUT

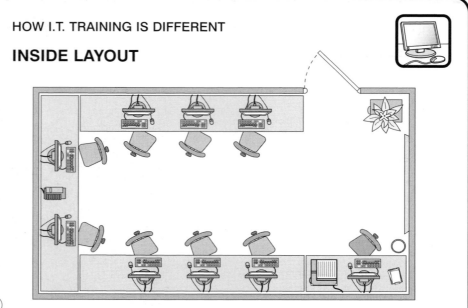

INSIDE LAYOUT

Pros

- Easy for users to switch attention between trainer-focus and PC focus (swivel chairs are, of course, essential for this)
- Easy for trainer to monitor learners' activities
- Few health and safety issues relating to power and networking

Cons

- Needs clear management by the trainer to avoid learner frustration if it is not clear where their attention should be at any time

TRAINING ROOM LAYOUT

Data Projectors

Where possible, projectors should be installed in the ceiling to avoid cabling issues. Beware window glare when using data projectors – the windows should be completely blacked out for best effect.

Technical versus Applications Training Layouts

Although not particularly good for applications training, where the trainer tends to need more regular sight of the learners' activities, the **classroom** layout can be a useful technical environment, particularly where two or more machines per learner are a necessary element. This layout provides for each individual to have their own working space.

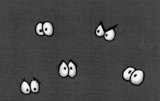

HOW I.T. TRAINING IS DIFFERENT

LEARNING-ENHANCING VISUAL MEDIA

Effective visuals add impact and interest. It's important however to use visual media that enhance learners' mastery of the session objectives. Used correctly, such media can aid learning, but used incorrectly, can distract or confuse the learner.

Media Use
Visual media can be two- or three-dimensional, or projected on a screen. The primary purposes of using media are to:

- Focus attention
- Aid understanding
- Add interest and stimulation
- Provide motivation for learning

HOW I.T. TRAINING IS DIFFERENT

MEDIA TYPES

The following lists the most commonly used media and major applications of each.

MEDIUM	APPLICATION AND FEATURES
Data projector	For pre-planned presentation or spontaneous demonstration Professional looking Graphics, text, colour, audio, video Presentations can be saved and published later
Flipchart	For pre-planned or spontaneous use Graphics, text, colour Can be retained, used as a chart or poster
Handouts/Job aids	Reference materials for 'on-the-job' processes Can contain pictures, charts, diagrams
Models/Real objects	Three-dimensional Hands-on opportunity
Overheads	Enlargement of any two-dimensional graphic Controlled pace of viewing

MEDIA TYPES

MEDIUM	APPLICATION AND FEATURES
Video	Used for processes that cannot readily be seen Realistic colour, motion and sound Can be purchased or internally produced
Whiteboard	For pre-planned or spontaneous use Graphics, text, colour Erasable/correctable
Electronic whiteboard	Application as above but with the benefit of printing
Interactive whiteboard	Enhances demonstration by clearly showing keystrokes, etc
Monitor splitter systems*	For real-time demonstration Graphics, text, colour Can be used to display an electronic presentation

*A combination of monitor splitters and switches provides a relatively low cost visual media option while allowing learners and trainers to switch between their own screens and the trainer's screens. This also allows the trainer to monitor the learners with complete discretion – make sure that the learners know that you are going to do this.

MEDIA HINTS AND TROUBLESHOOTING

- Provide one *main* idea for each visual
- Make sure that it is readable from everywhere in the room
- Use colour when possible, but bear in mind that some colours are hard to see
- Keep it simple for best effect
- Test all equipment in the training setting
- Don't use visual media just because they're available; they should enhance learning of session objectives
- When using online real-time examples or demonstrations, be sure you have a back-up if the system crashes
- Don't turn off a data projector until it has cooled down the bulb – the fan keeps running for some time after being turned to standby to do this. Turning it off too soon is a great way to blow the bulb, which can cost up to £500!

TYPES OF LEARNING EVENT

TYPES OF LEARNING EVENT

I.T. TRAINING EVENTS

IT training used to be classroom based, instructor-led and usually away from the working environment. Nowadays, this is only one of the ways in which IT training is delivered.

- **Trainer-led**

  Trainer-led training is still widely used, although often as part of the overall mix, with the emphasis being away from instruction and towards involvement.

- **Public Scheduled Course**

  Many training companies and internal departments offer 'public' courses open to anyone. These are often scheduled throughout a period to allow for individuals and organisations to plan their learning. They have the advantage of allowing learners to gain from a wide exposure to the subject from different perspectives but do not allow for individual or departmental issues to be dealt with.

- **Private Course**

  Organised at a date and time to suit the learners rather than the organisers, private courses allow for tailoring of the content to match the needs of the individuals or departments. This has the advantage of dealing only with the particular issue in hand but does not allow for exposure to other topics and ways of working.

TYPES OF LEARNING EVENT

GROUP LEARNING

Learning as part of a group is useful in order to see other perspectives and benefit from others' ways of working.

Size

The optimum group size for IT training is six to eight. Courses can be delivered to larger groups, but the ratio of trainer to learners dilutes the attention that any one learner can have and is best kept for courses where learners are less likely to need individual attention on a regular basis.

Dynamics

Group dynamics can have a great impact on the effectiveness of a course. A junior member of staff may feel intimidated working with more senior colleagues. A senior person may need to use IT to a lesser degree and may feel equally intimidated by their loss of status in an IT training environment, where a junior may have more skill or aptitude. A team being trained with its team leader may follow that leader rather than the trainer.

Awareness is the key to effective group management. If necessary, call a break and deal with issues arising on a one-to-one basis.

GROUP LEARNING

MIX AND PACE

The mix of skills on an IT training course can be difficult to manage. In other areas, individuals' experience or lack of it can add to the mix, but in IT training it is rarely anything but detrimental. The best way to avoid these issues is to ensure that prerequisite skills are determined prior to the course and that these have been met. Alternatively, schedule similar skill levels on the same course and match the pace of the group.

Although courses have objectives and both the learners and trainers know what needs to be covered, beware covering all the topics at all cost. Better to make sure that the important topics are covered fully (which may take more time than planned with some groups) than cover all topics and find that the learners can't remember any of them! Make sure that you know which topics **must** be covered.

Equally, there is no point in keeping learners who have clearly proved their learning.

TYPES OF LEARNING EVENT

GROUP LEARNING

MIX AND PACE

In reality, you are likely to get a mix of quicker and slower learners. To pace the course correctly, you need to consider:

- **The level of the course** – if the course is an advanced level and one of six learners does not have the prerequisite skill, it would not be right to pace the course to match them. By all means, work with them to build skills and confidence but not to the detriment of the learners who are on the right course with the right skills. If necessary, reschedule the learner onto a more suitable course.

- **The level of the group** – if only one learner in a group of six has actually achieved the prerequisites (and this is the worst possible situation), you may need to call on his or her good nature to allow you to work at a slower pace in order to train the group. Make sure that you offer extra hints, tips and traps so that the more skilled individual gets something back. Merely giving them extra exercises to allow the others to catch up does not benefit them, does it?

GROUP LEARNING

MIX AND PACE

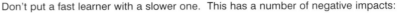

Don't put a fast learner with a slower one. This has a number of negative impacts:

- The fast learner may stop listening and learning, but simply pass on their potentially bad habits to the slower learner. After all, *you* are the trainer!
- The fast learner may feel 'used' and gain little from the experience
- The slower learner may feel intimidated and even more uncomfortable than they did on their own

Better still, put fast learners together and slower learners together:

- Fast learners can get extra tips and more challenging exercises to make them feel more valued, often working together in competitive fun
- Slower learners feel less alienated and more able to compare their understanding with that of someone with similar skills

ONE-TO-ONE LEARNING

An alternative to group learning, one-to-one offers individual support and training focused totally on the needs of the individual.

Asking them to bring along real-life files and issues they may need support with will make the experience of real value to the learner.

SUPPORTED LEARNING

Part of the learning blend is supported learning, previously known as distance learning, where workbooks provide the learning with the support of a telephone or postal tutor. This has now been overtaken by online learning.

Online Learning: Anything with a 'e' (for electronic) in front of it is associated with the internet and online working. E-learning has become a cost-effective, easy access method of self-paced learning delivery.

E-learning: Good e-learning packages combine the best of classroom learning with ease of access. It was initially over-hyped and under-delivered, but more recently the main e-learning providers have begun to develop effective learning tools, grounded in sound learning principles.

Web-based Learning: Many e-learning applications are delivered via an intranet or the internet. Intranet-based applications allow for secure information to be delivered quickly over existing networks. Internet-based applications rely on fast, reliable internet connections, which is proving to be a limiting factor in e-learning design.

SUPPORTED LEARNING

Computer-based Learning: Delivering learning via a PC through the use of a CD or DVD is popular. Internet and intranet delivery allows multiple learners to access the same learning simultaneously; computer-based training (CBT) allows only a single user. It is, though, quick and easy to access, not requiring network connection.

E-tutoring: Used to support online learning, e-tutoring ranges from e-mail support, forum and discussion board moderating to online, synchronous meetings and chats. The skills of an e-tutor differ little from those of a trainer, as both need to juggle a number of different balls at the same time, but the balls differ in both environments. The most obvious difference is that rapport-building skills are missing from this faceless environment.

If you want to find out what being an e-tutor is like, enrol on an e-learning course. Then consider what the tutor has to do and how they do it. Good e-tutors combine rapport building, coaching and assessment of learning with the necessary course administration seamlessly, often with the help of a good Learning Management System.

SUPPORTED LEARNING

Learning Management System (LMS)

An LMS provides a framework for delivery of e-learning and can help management of:

- Content – this can be easily and quickly updated, meaning that little time is wasted in maintaining the most up-to-date information
- Pre- and post-learning tests – which can be administered through practice tests and assessment
- Ongoing assignments – can be tracked and progress monitored
- Communication and collaborative working – one of the most important elements of good e-tutoring, this can be facilitated by using online discussion boards, chats and virtual classrooms

Virtual Classrooms

These are used for the delivery of virtual training. E-training is different from e-tutoring. A good e-trainer delivers training, almost as in a classroom, but using online tools. This is often in real-time, which provides interaction through real-time chat rooms and voice and video communication, but can also be recorded for playback at a later date.

STRUCTURE OF LEARNING EVENTS

STRUCTURE OF LEARNING EVENTS

PRIMACY AND RECENCY

Research shows that we remember the first (**primary**) things we hear or see, the last (**recent**) things we hear or see and any **unique** elements in between. Other than that, our attention fades. To make learning effective, therefore, we need to be **PRU**dent. Remember: *'Tell them what you are going to tell them, tell them and then tell them what you have told them'*. Try doing something different in the middle bit to ensure uniqueness.

All learning events, whether they be five days of classroom training or one hour of online learning, have a beginning, middle and end.

The three '**L**'ements:
- Lighting the Way to Learning
- The Learning itself
- Laying Down the Learning for the Future

Each learning '**L**' ement comprises one or more learning points. This allows for the content to be broken down into manageable 'chunks'. Each of these learning points also has these three '**L**' ements so that the event builds in a logical learning sequence.

STRUCTURE OF LEARNING EVENTS

LIGHTING THE WAY
FEATURES AND BENEFITS

Learners have many different motivators. So some of your learners will be excited, while others will feel unsure and even intimidated by technology. This is your chance to make them feel comfortable and to see the benefits of their learning.

Informing learners of the **features** they will learn does not give them the **benefits**. If you are unsure of the benefits of a particular feature, ask yourself: '*So what?*' when describing the feature.

For example, in a session to learn about an e-mail product, one of the features might be that you can send an e-mail to multiple addresses at the same time. So what? Ask yourself that question and you will find many different answers, dependent on why someone might want to send an e-mail in the first place. Keep asking yourself the question to keep benefits at the forefront of motivation.

You can't possibly know the benefits of each learning point for each individual, so there is no sense in trying to tell them. Your job here is to let them know what features they are going to be learning about in general terms, and then ask them to think about how this might benefit them in their world.

LIGHTING THE WAY

OBJECTIVES

All learning points should have a clear objective.

An objective is the destination for the learning point – the thing you are lighting the way towards. It describes the action the learners will be able to carry out or the behaviour they will display at the end of the learning point. Objectives should conform to the **SMARTER** principle:

S pecific – clear and unambiguous wording.

M easurable – you need a measure to 'test' against. Otherwise, how will they (or you) know that they have achieved it?

A chievable – an unachievable objective is pointless. An alternative 'A' is Agreed. It is important that the learners agree to meet the objective as you don't want to force something on them.

R ealistic – learners want to know that this is going to benefit them in the real world.

T imed – this ties in with 'measurable' above, as time is one of the measures you can use.

E njoyable – it helps to motivate learners to achieve the objective when they enjoy both the journey and the achievement.

R elevant – to the needs of both the learner and their organisation.

LIGHTING THE WAY

HOW TO WRITE OBJECTIVES

Objectives should always be positively phrased – state what is going to **occur** not what is going to be **avoided** by the new learning. Make sure that objectives are also understandable – don't use 50 words when 10 will do.

To help with this, write objectives that are made up of the following:

Action
The action or behaviour change required, expressed in the form of a verb. Beginning objectives with the following phrase helps, as it forces a verb:

'By the end of this session you will be able to …'

Notice that the structure of this phrase, '**you *will* be able to**' expresses your confidence in their ability to learn and your ability to facilitate that. This is reassuring for the less confident learners.

LIGHTING THE WAY

HOW TO WRITE OBJECTIVES (Cont'd)

Level

This is the level to which the action will occur. For example, it is possible to '*set up user accounts*' in at least two ways – correctly and incorrectly (with lots of variations in between). Also, it is neither specific nor measurable to set up user accounts without knowing how many would be considered acceptable.

In the case above, you could say: '*set up at least three users accounts correctly*'. The expression *at least* allows for the more able to set up more than three while making sure that the objective is achievable for everyone.

So, '*by the end of this session you will be able to set up at least three user accounts correctly*' allows both you and the learners to know what they are going to achieve and how they will know when they get there.

LIGHTING THE WAY

HOW WILL I LEARN?

Adult learners are best motivated to learn when they are clear about what is going to happen to them.

It is important, when lighting the way, to shine the light on the Learning section of the journey. For example, we may discuss the topic, then show the learners how it works by 'holding their hands' through the process, then allow them to practise before undertaking a final exercise.

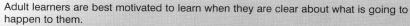
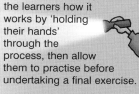

STRUCTURE OF LEARNING EVENTS

THE LEARNING 'L' EMENT

LECTURE

There are many different learning delivery methods available to the IT trainer.

Although the least interactive learning delivery method, **lecture** (the trainer delivering learning material verbally) does have its place in IT training, particularly when introducing new material. Telling the learners, however, should be a small part of the overall training delivery. While it is quicker and easier to tell rather than help the learners find out, being told is a far less effective way to learn.

Lectures should be full of **FSSS**:

- **F**ocused – on the topic
- **S**hort – involve learners as soon as possible
- **S**timulating – ask yourself, *'Would I want to listen to this?'*
- **S**upported – by visual or other learning aids

THE LEARNING 'L' EMENT

DISCUSSION

Discussion is a useful delivery method when a topic or skill has already been introduced. It is highly interactive and provides a stimulus for learners to consider the benefits of the topic, function or skill as well as its potential limitations and, in particular, how it will affect them as individuals. Discussions are very easy to lose track of and need to be handled skilfully.

Discussions should be:

- Pre-planned – you need to know what you want to achieve from the discussion and how you intend to steer the discussion towards achieving it

- Managed – make sure that everyone gets their say and that the discussion does not get hijacked

- Timed – plan the discussion and make an accurate assessment of the time required

THE LEARNING 'L' EMENT

ANTI-DEMONSTRATION

This is not a demonstration against the learning, but the opposite of the sort of demonstration where the trainer shows and tells the learner who does nothing but watch and listen. An **anti-demonstration** allows the trainer to show the learners in a safe environment (particularly useful where learners could damage a system by getting it wrong).

Learners 'lead' the trainer through the demonstration. As a trainer, you only go where the learners tell you to (unless, of course, that would be disastrous). Think of the *Golden Shot* or Saturday morning children's TV where a caller guides a celebrity to aim at a target.

Anti-demonstrations should be:

- Chunked – into manageable bites to avoid overload
- Interactive – the learners are in charge
- Followed – by the learners doing what they have just demonstrated to themselves

THE LEARNING 'L' EMENT

WALK-THROUGH

This is where the trainer takes the whole group, step-by-step, through a process. Each learner is doing the same thing at the same time and the steps are explained along the way with a combination of asking and telling the learners.

Walk-throughs should be:

- Chunked – into manageable bites to avoid overload

- Logical – good for learning processes

- Learner-focused – avoid telling when asking will achieve the same result

123 CLICK!
456 DRAG!

THE LEARNING 'L' EMENT

HANDS-ON AND COACHING

Hands-on

Once a new process has been:

- **Introduced**, eg: through lecture
- **Considered**, eg: through discussion
- **Shown**, eg: through an anti-demonstration
- **Done**, eg: through a walk-through

the learners can get some free **hands-on** practice to consolidate the learning.

When designing hands-on practice tasks make sure that they are similar enough to the walk-through or anti-demonstration tasks to avoid confusion, yet sufficiently different to avoid boredom or brain shutdown.

Coaching

One-to-one or small group **coaching** involves working with learners to extend or enhance existing skills, during hands-on practice. Again, the importance of questions is evident as many learners require coaching as much to build confidence as to build skills.

THE LEARNING 'L' EMENT

RECAPPING

An essential part, both within the individual 'L' ements and throughout the learning event, is **recap**. Use questions to check understanding. Better still, get learners to devise their own questions for each other on an ongoing basis.

Be creative about recapping learning. Ask the learners to write down three things from an earlier session they will be able to use in their work. Then ask them to choose their favourite parlour game – *charades, hangman, 20 questions*, etc. Pair up the learners and ask them to work out their partner's three things using their chosen parlour game as the communication method.

This has many benefits – the learners first have to think about what they learned and its use, then they have to represent that to another person (with hilarious results when someone uses charades to represent an obscure technical concept). They then have to play the game in reverse, working out their partner's topics, so they have to think again about what was learned. On top of all that, they are away from the PCs and often laughing and relaxing while learning – what more could you want?

THE LEARNING 'L' EMENT

CHECKING THE CHANGE

The final part of the learning 'L' ement itself is to check that the learning has taken place. **Test** the learning by setting an exercise for the learners to carry out that can be measured against the objective set out at the start of the session.

The learners don't need to think of this as a test (be creative and find an alternative name for this exercise), but it is important that the learning is truly tested in order to be able to confirm each individual's state in relation to the objective. Only then can relevant post-course coaching and support be offered, where necessary.

Also referred to as assessment, tests should be:
Clear   – unambiguous instructions
Individual   – you need to know whether each individual has achieved
Appropriate – to the learning objective
Objective   – success criteria must be easily recognised

Remember… before you say goodbye, say **CIAO**.

LAYING DOWN THE LEARNING

TRANSFER OF LEARNING

Learning is only of benefit when it is **transferred** out of the classroom and into the real world. Make sure that the learners are thinking about WIIFM as early as possible in the session and continue it throughout. Get them to write it down, speak it and demonstrate it wherever possible to ensure full exposure.

Very few of us are able to see this transfer back in the learning environment but, when the opportunity arises, there are numerous post-course support options and support materials available to help.

LAYING DOWN THE LEARNING

POST-COURSE SUPPORT

Floorwalking

Floorwalking is particularly useful *after* a formal learning event, but can be used *instead of* one. It involves a trainer literally walking the floor where the learner is working to coach learners in their real world applications and the issues surrounding them.

This is often unplanned coaching, delivered at the learner's workstation. It involves a learner 'bumping into' a trainer or going in search of one they know is around on a particular day. Where development issues are known, it is useful for a floorwalker to *plan* the day by making short (15-30 minute) blocks of time available for people to book during the day. The trainer then goes to the learner's workstation at the allotted time.

Surgeries

Used for longer one-to-one or small group coaching sessions, surgery appointments are pre-booked and are often held away from the learner's workstation, perhaps in a side room. This allows for the learner to gain from the coaching away from the distractions found in many open-plan environments.

STRUCTURE OF LEARNING EVENTS

LAYING DOWN THE LEARNING

POST-COURSE SUPPORT

IT Helpdesk

IT Helpdesks often keep records of calls and this information, if collected and available to trainers, is invaluable for helping users through on-the-job coaching and support. It may even identify someone who needs further training.

Develop links with IT Helpdesk staff to fully benefit the organisation by working together to reduce user problems.

Forums

Internet or intranet forums are a great way of ensuring that everyone has access to best practice, questions and answers, etc. Rather than offering an individual service, in which the same question could be answered hundreds of times, get users to post their questions to a forum, where other users and trainers can provide answers and share experience.

It is important that this is a managed process, however, as potential abuse could lead to the facility being removed and the benefit being lost.

STRUCTURE OF LEARNING EVENTS

SUPPORT MATERIALS

Courseware
Used as part of the course delivery, this is often in the form of workbooks for learners to work through. Detailed background information manuals, that often gather dust or keep doors open, are less common with the development of good, user-friendly online help.

Quick Reference Guides
Providing just the 'How the heck do I ...?' information, quick reference guides are often produced for the learners to take away and access quickly the information they need on a regular basis. Make sure that these guides are as easy to carry and read as possible to ensure that they are used.

Help Screens
It is useful to build information on accessing online help into a training session. At the very least make sure that the learners know that there is help available and how they can get it. The more they can help themselves, the more meaningful that help is going to be in the future.

FACILITATING LEARNING

FACILITATING LEARNING

LEARNER-CENTRED TECHNIQUES

Facilitating learning changes the focus from the trainer to the learner. There are numerous learner-centred techniques that will embed the focus.

Asking questions is an essential part of the work of a trainer to ensure involvement and interaction, test understanding and build rapport. Use questions to find out not only what your learners know, but also what they don't know that they know.

Learners may believe that they have little or no knowledge of the topic being trained, yet skilful questioning can not only make them, and you, understand how their existing knowledge fits with the new skill being trained, it can also build confidence and reduce barriers to learning.

FACILITATING LEARNING

TYPES OF QUESTIONING

There are many different types of question, each suited to particular situations:

- Use **closed** questions when you need to check understanding of a process or task with a right or wrong answer:
  'How many records are in the database?'

- Use **open** questions when you need to find out about underlying knowledge and understanding:
  'Why is it useful to know how many records are in the database?'

- Use **leading** questions to build confidence and assist learners:
  'If you want to add a new record, which item on the record menu do you think you should select?'

- Use **probing** questions to clarify or build on partial answers:
  'That's right, it is ADD, so now where do you think you should go to add a new record?'

To be truly learner-centred, questions should form the basis of your training.

ASKING QUESTIONS

As well as many different types of question, there are also many different ways of asking questions.

Group Questions

These are thrown open to the whole group to answer – the majority of trainers' questions are likely to fall into this category. Any one or more of the learners can answer.

Individual Questions

The most effective way of asking an individual is to ask a group question and then direct the question to an individual. Using the name first is more direct, but instantly excludes all the other learners in the room. They may not even listen to the question, let alone think about the answer, once they hear someone else's name.

With the former technique, all learners get the opportunity to think of the answer, if only for a split second, giving them the chance to reinforce their learning or learn something new.

ASKING QUESTIONS

Round Robin Questions
Used to get different answers to the same question
– often in introductions or when wanting to find
out each individual's take on an issue.

Try to avoid going around the learners in
sequence, as they then concentrate on their
own answer and don't listen to the others,
knowing when their turn will be. If you
request answers randomly all the learners
have to stay on the ball and listen to
everyone else in case they are next.

Make sure, however, that this is not
intimidating – it can be quite fun (try
Spin the Bottle).

FACILITATING LEARNING

BEING ASKED QUESTIONS

There are three ways of dealing with learners' questions:

Answer it
Often the first option, this should actually be the last!

Reflect it
If someone can articulate the question, they may well know the answer, or at least know more than they think they do. Reflecting it back to the learner allows them to reconsider the question (you may need to help a little) and can be a big confidence boost when they realise they know the answer. Many questions are asked in order to confirm understanding not to gain it. Be sensitive when doing this. Be careful not to put the learner under so much pressure that they dare not ask another question.

Deflect it
Where a learner has asked a question, and you have reflected it back to them appropriately, a further option is to deflect it back to the rest of the group. This is an effective way of involving everyone and recognising the skill and knowledge of the whole group. Once again, sensitivity is the key as it may undermine the original questioner's confidence if a question is deflected inappropriately.

FACILITATING LEARNING

LISTENING SKILLS

Of course, asking questions is only half of the story – you then need to *listen* to the answers. Make sure that your learners know you are listening by using active listening techniques.

Use non-verbal communication (eg: nods, strong eye contact) together with verbal recognition signals such as '*yes*' and '*OK*'.

Paraphrase communications to ensure your understanding is correct: '*So, what you are saying is …*'

Ask probing questions to clarify or expand an answer. This can be done simply by using the word: '*And …?*' or when dealing with processes: '*And then …?*'.

ACCELERATING LEARNING

This is not about making people learn faster, but actually about making them learn **deeper**. Make it real for the learners.

Get them to create their own exercises. Ask them to design an exercise for a colleague or to set a question for the recap session. Not only does it mean that their brains are working on what you want them to, but involving the learners will make the experience more real for them. There is little worse than having something inflicted on you by an external source (you in this case).

Make sure that the learners are clear about where they are going (what their objectives are) and how they will recognise it when they get there.

Processes can be trained using *Day in the Life Of* … techniques, where a real-life process is replicated in the training environment. Rather than the event being theory that then has to be transferred to the real world, the real world is simulated in the learning environment, thereby reducing the transfer time and accelerating the learning.

USING THE BRAIN

The brain comprises a complex network of nerve cells and transmitters that respond to stimuli received from the senses. Imagine the brain as a rolling Victorian landscape of fields, hills, trees, streams. Navigating this landscape is not easy, as there are many different routes to take – over hills, across streams, between trees. So where do you start? Well, tentatively, at first, feeling your way to make sure that you have the information you need to get from A to B. You may even have to turn back or change direction if you make a mistake on your way.

How will you feel the next time you have to make the journey? Probably a little more confident, but still wary because the path is not yet worn enough. The more often you make the journey, however, the more worn the path becomes and the easier and quicker it is to travel. You may build bridges across the streams and tunnels beneath the hills. You may even attach ropes to the trees and hang on for dear life!

This is learning – **the more the neural pathways are worn, the more permanent the learning**. Beware: this applies equally to known information and can make unlearning an old habit in order to learn something new more difficult than starting from scratch.

FACILITATING LEARNING

USING THE BRAIN

To make learning stick, you need to make sure that pathways are trodden in as many ways as possible. When introducing new topics, **link to known topics** to add to an already wearing pathway. Where old knowledge needs to be unlearned, avoid linking the new knowledge, but make sure that the old is given equal stature. Being told that what we know is no longer valid is a sure-fire way of increasing resistance to change.

Where the old system is well-loved and you sense resistance, allow the learners to value it alongside the new. Try asking them to consider the following questions:

The best thing about the old system is...
The worst thing about the old system is...

This will lead them to express affection for the old system, while accepting its weaknesses.

If the new system developers have done their job, they will not have lost any of the good but will have worked at getting rid of the bad. So, you can sell the benefits of the new system by letting them know that the things on their 'best' list are still there (although the process may have changed) and the things on their 'worst' list have gone. Your understanding of their affection for the old will build and maintain rapport.

FACILITATING LEARNING

CREATIVITY

There is no reason why we cannot be as creative in IT training as in 'soft' skills training. When it comes to making learning stick, dry, technical subjects are best presented in a creative way. IT often takes itself too seriously and this can create barriers between IT 'techies' and IT users.

What's wrong with having some fun? As long as we are not playing games for the sake of it, introducing some fun into training is a great way to stimulate those brainwaves!

We tend to remember the first things we hear or see and also the last things. We also remember **unique** elements and these are often the fun things we can do to make a difference.

Make sure that you are not having your own fun at the expense of the learners and that the fun things you do are linked to the learning objective, then go for it!

CREATIVE TOOLS AND TECHNIQUES
ANALOGY

One of the sharpest tools in any IT trainer's toolkit, analogy is about making an abstract process or function real in terms of the learners' understanding. When considering analogies, try to find something that most people can relate to – think of them, not you. One example of this is a tool used for applying formatting from existing text to new text – it is like dipping a brush into a paint pot and then brushing it over a wall.

Analogies can be:

- **Expanded** making sure you select the right paint pot before dipping your brush
- **Extended** double-dipping is a progression with the formatting tool, and
- **Reinforced** making up a rhyme or song (perhaps *dippady doo dah!*)

throughout the session to make sure that the learning sticks.

Avoid using your own analogies all the time, though, as learners' own analogies are going to be far stronger for them. Get them to make up their own – perhaps as a recap game with a partner. The sillier the analogy the more it is likely to be remembered.

CREATIVE TOOLS AND TECHNIQUES

EXPERIENTIAL STORIES

Making learning real by the use of stories is a powerful tool. Stories make people relax and listen, putting the brain into its optimum learning state. Story-telling is an art form at its best, but even the least talented of us can help learners understand by telling them about '*the time when …*'. Use stories from your own experience, or just be creative.

This is useful where you know that they may struggle with the topic being learned. You know this because you struggled yourself. Don't say: '*This is going to be hard but don't worry, if I can do it, you can*'. The brain can't cope with interpreting negatives without going there. The mere fact that you have told them it will be hard will make them believe it is. Telling them not to worry implies that they have something to worry about! You now have a group of very apprehensive learners who are only feeling that way because you tried to reassure them.

Instead, try telling them about some of the issues you overcame when learning this, **how** you overcame them and what the **benefits** of overcoming them were.

FACILITATING LEARNING

CREATIVE TOOLS AND TECHNIQUES
ACRONYMS AND PROPS

Acronyms
The acronyms referred to here are not jargon, but the ones designed to help make the learning stick. Once again, the best ideas will come from the learners themselves, although you may offer your suggestions. Remember *Every Good Boy Deserves Favour*? My version is *Every Green Bucket Deserves Fish* – makes far more sense to me as I picture a green bucket with fish swimming around in it!

Props
One of my favourite props is a magic wand. I use this to add a fun element to the training and learners can borrow it whenever they need an injection of magic. Often, towards the end of the day, when learners are getting tired, they come to borrow the wand and wave it over their final exercise.

Other props include modelling putty, which is useful to have around to prevent the kinaesthetic activists fiddling with their PCs. They can make relevant models or just play with the putty while listening or watching.

Use props to add to a story you are telling or ask learners to find the connection between a prop and a learned topic.

CREATIVE TOOLS AND TECHNIQUES
THEMES

What about setting up an overall learning event around a particular theme? A journey could begin with the joining instructions being sent in the form of a travel ticket, being checked-in on arrival and with a room decorated appropriately for an overseas destination. The training delivery element can then follow the theme and this continues into the post-course support, with help available from the travel guide or flight controller.

Or send out joining instructions in the form of an invitation to a party. Have a party bag on the desk on arrival, containing notepad, pen, exercise disk, quick reference guide, etc (and a lollipop, of course).

Or start by changing the user logons to something a little more creative than 'Trainee one', 'Trainee two', which is the case in most training rooms. For e-mail training, what about setting up characters that pair up together, such as Starsky and Hutch, Tom and Jerry, Dick Dastardly and Muttley, Rodney and Del Boy Trotter, Morecambe and Wise, (beware copyright issues when using copyright characters). Or set up fictional Happy Families or other popular characters. Ask the learners, when they send messages to their partners, to do so in character.

CREATIVE TOOLS AND TECHNIQUES

GAMES

Games should only be used where they enhance the learning, not for the sake of it, as they might detract. No one should be forced to join in. If you refer to *playing a game* you may get some resistance from some learners, while others will relish the prospect of some light relief. Think about the words you use when introducing a game; calling it a *light-hearted recap exercise* might help the traditionalists while letting the others know that it will also be fun.

Where an exercise allows for some self-expression in the final result, try musical chairs. This will get people to move to another person's seat and look at their work to see how they did it, question them about the techniques used, etc. This is much more fun than just asking learners to talk to their neighbours.

CREATIVE TOOLS AND TECHNIQUES

GAMES

Pass the parcel can be used as a recap method. Ask each person to write down three questions about the preceding session(s) and use the sheets of paper as wrapping for a chocolate or other treat in the centre. Pass these parcels around the room to music and when the music stops, each person unwraps a layer from the parcel in their hands at the time and answers the question. The final layer, of course, contains the treat.

Use multiple intelligences to enhance learning. Ask learners, in groups, to make up a short story, rhyme or song, encompassing the main learning points of the day or course. Ask them to describe a topic as if it were an animal, stating why that animal would be appropriate. For example, '*I think that the help feature in this application is like a parrot, because it is bright and colourful and keeps telling me what to do*'.

CREATIVE TOOLS AND TECHNIQUES

MUSIC

Some of the previous suggestions incorporate music, but even on its own music can lead to a relaxing atmosphere, conducive to learning. Picture the scene … you walk into a brightly decorated training room to be greeted by a smiling, confident trainer who welcomes you with pleasant, upbeat music playing in the background. Wouldn't that make you feel better than the alternative of a grey-green room, with a trainer rushing around doing last-minute preparations, who sits you in front of a PC in silence, next to the other man who came in early and is now looking around him wishing he hadn't?

Apart from the fact that the right music can enhance learning by creating an appropriate brainwave state, it can also enhance (or detract from, dependent on the choice of music) the overall event by setting the mood.

You must obtain a Performing Rights Society music licence to be able to play music in public and there may be other copyright issues you need to be aware of in your particular location, so check first.

EVALUATING LEARNING

INTRODUCTION

Evaluating learning is divided into two main camps and they are often at odds with each other within an organisation:

- Evaluating the learning event
- Evaluating the learner's workplace effectiveness

Historically, trainers have only been concerned with evaluating the learning event: were the learners *happy* with the experience? The expression *happy sheet* will be familiar to most of us. It is important, however, within the event itself to evaluate the actual skills or behaviour change. This is usually done by *testing* the learner against the learning objective.

Once the learning event is over, few trainers get involved in evaluating the increased effectiveness of the learner back in the workplace. This is seen as the department's or organisation's role. Supportive managers who are aware of their staff needs, make sure that the correct learning is made available and are actively involved in the transfer of the skills into the workplace are super-heroes! They are also few and far between in the pressurised environments in which they often find themselves.

EVALUATING LEARNING

TRANSFER OF LEARNING

It is important that the trainer is aware of the learner's needs in the widest business context, as well as at an individual skill level, and sets up strategies for transfer of learning to the workplace from the start of the learning event. This can be done by:

● The use of real-life scenarios or case studies
● Exercises to help users think about why they might use the application or tool at work
● Idea sharing within the learning event: you would be surprised how many times someone says: *'What a great idea. I could use that for ...'*

As part of a consolidation exercise, ask learners to make a list: *'I will take and use from this workshop ...'*. This will encourage them to think about not only what they will use but why, where and when the learning will be useful to them.

EVALUATING LEARNING

TRANSFER OF LEARNING

After the event itself, consider setting up a group forum, perhaps on the organisation's intranet, where ideas and challenges can be aired and shared. Once set in motion, these things often find their own momentum and need little facilitation.

Where possible, go back to the learners at defined periods after the event to evaluate the learning within the workplace. Most managers will be pleased to see you, as they are probably not super-heroes but are aware of their requirement to be so. This can also help you with training programme planning as you can clearly see the needs within the organisation without having to be told what people *think* they need.

EVALUATING LEARNING

KIRKPATRICK'S FOUR LEVELS

Donald Kirkpatrick (1967) defined what is arguably the most widely-used approach to evaluation. His four-level model is simple, flexible and complete and, although extensively developed, has never been bettered.

Level 1: Evaluating Reaction
- Happy sheets
- Verbal and non-verbal feedback

Level 2: Evaluating Learning
- Pre- and post-course 'tests'
- On-course exercises/questions

Level 3: Evaluating Behaviour
- On-the-job observation/interviews
- Manager/peer feedback

Level 4: Evaluating Results
- Management information/statistical data
- Performance against objectives

EVALUATING LEARNING

KIRKPATRICK'S FOUR LEVELS

Most trainers evaluate at **Reaction level** (Level 1).

Most trainers evaluate at **Learning level** (Level 2) through on-course exercises and tests but few trainers test learning pre- and post-course.

Very few trainers evaluate training at **Behaviour level** (Level 3) through proactive post-course workplace transfer of learning.

Even fewer (if any) are involved in **Results level** (Level 4) evaluation.

To get the best out of this model, trainers need to integrate as many levels as possible into as many evaluation methods as possible. It is possible to include learning and transfer of learning evaluation in Reaction level questionnaires. For example, including questions such as: *'List 3 ways in which this learning is going to improve your performance at work'* links your Reaction level questionnaire to the Behaviour level and this information can be used in any post-course discussions.

About the Author

Jooli Atkins, BSc (Hons), MCIM, Lic CIPD, MITOL, MIITT
Jooli has been working in IT, mostly in training, since 1982 and writes from first-hand experience as a training practitioner and project manager. She has been responsible for managing and delivering the successful transfer of IT skills on many national projects, notably the Royal Borough of Kensington and Chelsea Council, where 2,200 users were upgraded to a new software version, in just 2 months, through the use of roadshows, floorwalking and online reference materials. Most recently, she managed a project for National Grid Gas that won the Bronze Award in the Institute of IT Training Internal Training Project of the Year category in 2006. Jooli works closely with the Institute of IT Training and the British Computer Society in raising the profile of IT training within the IT delivery cycle.

Matrix FortyTwo's Excellent Learning Facilitation programme has recently gained industry recognition and has grown in popularity over the past few years. Learning events from this programme help the ideas in this book come to life for trainers and subject-matter experts.

Contact
Jooli can be contacted at Matrix FortyTwo, 8-9 George's Place, Pocklington, East Yorkshire, YO42 2DF Email: jooli@matrix42.co.uk

ORDER FORM

Your details

Name _____

Position _____

Company _____

Address _____

_____

_____

Telephone _____

Fax _____

E-mail _____

VAT No. (EC companies) _____

Your Order Ref _____

Please send me:

		No. copies
The I.T. Trainer's	Pocketbook	
The _____	Pocketbook	
The _____	Pocketbook	
The _____	Pocketbook	
The _____	Pocketbook	

Order by Post

MANAGEMENT POCKETBOOKS LTD

LAUREL HOUSE, STATION APPROACH,
ALRESFORD, HAMPSHIRE SO24 9JH UK

Order by Phone, Fax or Internet

Telephone: +44 (0)1962 735573
Facsimile: +44 (0)1962 733637
E-mail: sales@pocketbook.co.uk
Web: www.pocketbook.co.uk

MANAGEMENT POCKETBOOKS